Giant
of the
Deep

GW00707579

Contents

Features

Fully grown live giant squid have never been studied, but they do exist. Read all about it in **Giant Catch!** on page 5.

A team in the Antarctic is following a giant iceberg as it breaks from the ice shelf and floats into the open sea. Join them on page 7.

Many ocean creatures are clever at hiding themselves. See how successful you are at blending into the background in **Hide and See** on page 23.

People have hunted whales for centuries, but today many people believe it should be banned forever. Read some of the arguments on page 27 and make your own decision.

What is a commonly found fossil?

Visit **www.infosteps.co.uk**
for more about **SHARKS.**

Fearsome Beasts

Long ago sailors often came home from their ocean voyages with strange tales of fearsome sea monsters. They told stories of creatures with tentacles 18 metres long that reached up out of the sea to devour their ships. They spoke of gigantic beasts that heaved ships into the air and then used their long arms to crush the ships. What were these creatures?

IN THE NEWS

Giant Catch!

Steve O'Shea, a marine biologist in New Zealand, knows more about giant squid than anyone else in the world. So when a fishing boat hauled up a dead squid that measured 11 metres yesterday, Dr O'Shea was called.

Giant squid live in the deep sea, but they come closer to the surface to breed. Dr O'Shea has examined nearly 100 dead giant squid, but no one has yet been able to study a live adult giant squid.

To this day the oceans' depths hold many mysteries. However, we know now that giant squid and octopuses do live **fathoms** deep. We know that giant jellyfish and sea stars live far below the surface. We know that the blue whale is the largest living creature on our planet and we have learned a lot about the other giants that inhabit the oceans.

Giant octopuses were once thought to be fearsome, but now we know they are shy and gentle.

Breakers and Bergs

Monster waves have terrified sailors for centuries and provided material for many books and movies. Scientists have now discovered that giant waves are created in a storm when slow-moving waves are caught up by a series of faster-moving waves travelling at twice the speed. The waves pile on top of each other to create one gigantic wave that can be up to 37 metres high! These huge waves are capable of breaking a large ship in half and sending it to the bottom of the ocean in minutes.

Icebergs could also be described as ocean giants. Icebergs are created when chunks of **pack ice** break free and float off into open sea. They are especially common in the Arctic and Antarctic Oceans. Sailors must take care when travelling through iceberg-filled waters, and ships that sail in polar seas usually have a specially made **hull** so that they are very strong.

Enormous waves are thought to be behind the sudden disappearance of many ships.

When this iceberg first broke away, it had a surface area of 11,655 square kilometres!

On March 17, 2000 a satellite recorded a giant iceberg breaking away from the Ross Ice Shelf in Antarctica. In January 2001, a team of divers and scientists, a boat crew and a helicopter set off for the Antarctic to study that iceberg and see what would happen to it. They were amazed to discover that large colonies of seals and birds made their home on the iceberg. Algae also grew on the submerged parts of the iceberg, providing food for some fish and other small animals. The research team realized that icebergs are an important part of the polar ocean ecosystem.

The research ship

Great Cetaceans

Whales, like dolphins and porpoises, are cetaceans. Cetaceans are mammals, not fish. Although they have fins and tails and spend all their lives in water, whales have lungs and need to breathe air just like we do. Their blowholes are like noses on the top of their heads so they can breathe without coming very far out of the water. There are more than 80 different species of cetaceans and some of them are truly giants of the deep.

Whales communicate with each other by making sounds. Sound can travel about 2 kilometres per second underwater, so in the right conditions, whales can communicate with each other over great distances.

Orca

Blue whale

Sperm whale

Humpback whale

Grey whale

Southern right whale

Once about 10,000 beluga whales lived in Canada's St Lawrence River. Now the population is estimated to be only about 700. A study has found that the main cause of this drop is river pollution. Many industries dump chemical waste straight into the river, and because of this the belugas' health is very poor. The government is working to reduce the pollution and improve the whales' habitat.

A whale can be recognized by the shape of its waterspout and the shape of its tail.

Blue whale

Orca

Beluga whales

Toothed Whales and Baleen Whales

All whales are meat eaters. Most toothed whales use their teeth to catch their food. Then they just suck it down   not many species chew their food first! Orca have clever hunting patterns and work together as a group to catch their prey. Beluga whales use **echolocation** to find their food.

Baleen whales are the biggest creatures in the ocean yet they eat some of the smallest—krill and tiny plankton. Different species of baleen whale have different ways of eating krill. The fin whale skims the water and gulps as it swims, while the grey whale stirs up mud on the ocean floor to capture small crustaceans and worms. Humpback whales work together to catch fish.

Humpback whales swim around a school of fish in a slow spiralling circle, blowing a "net" of bubbles. As the fish become confused and trapped by the bubbles they swim closer and closer together. Then the humpbacks simply open their mouths and suck them in!

A fin whale feeding

Beluga whales use low echolocation clicks spaced well apart to scan the ice-filled waters where they live. Once a whale picks up the presence of a fish it starts moving in on its target. The clicks become faster and faster, ending in a long creak.

Plankton

Humpback whales

Krill

Bats of the Sea

Rays and skates have huge flat fins that look a lot like bats' wings. Because of this the family of rays and skates are called batoids.

Rays and skates are close relatives of sharks. Like sharks, rays have flexible skeletons of **cartilage** instead of bone. Their bodies are specially suited to feeding on the sea floor where most of them live.

The giant of the ray family is the manta ray. It can be as large as 7 metres from fin to fin. Most rays have a thin spiked tail that often has a poisonous **barb**. Some rays can deliver a nasty shock with their tails.

The manta ray eats plankton. It feeds constantly by looping through clouds of plankton.

Bluespotted ribbontail ray

Members of the Batoid Family

Ray

Skate

Guitarfish

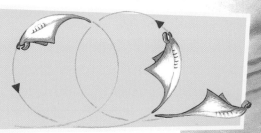

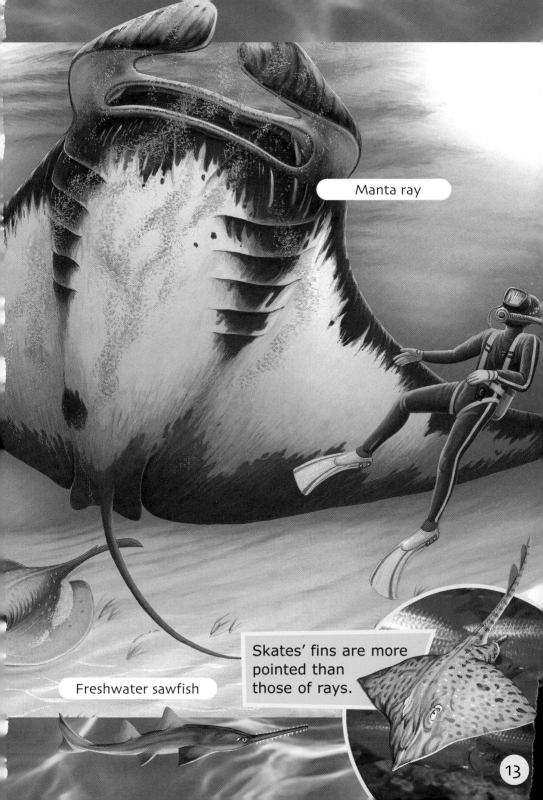

Manta ray

Skates' fins are more pointed than those of rays.

Freshwater sawfish

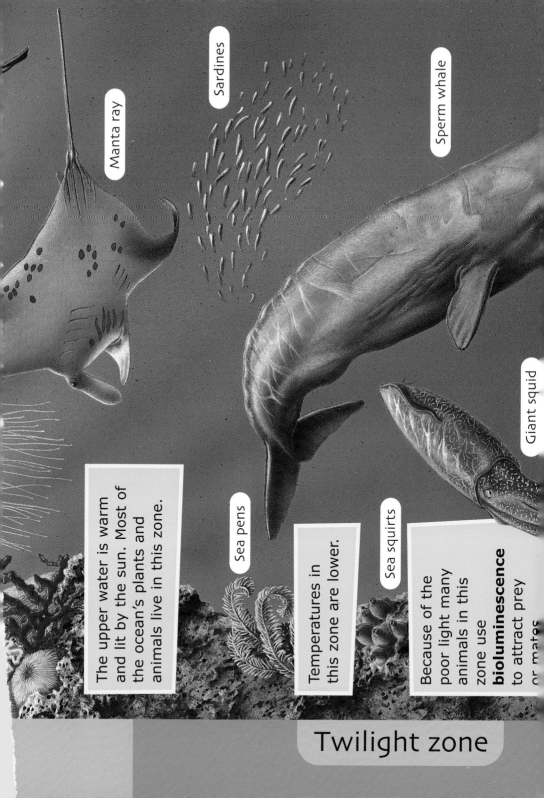

Manta ray

Sardines

Sperm whale

Giant squid

Sea pens

Sea squirts

The upper water is warm and lit by the sun. Most of the ocean's plants and animals live in this zone.

Temperatures in this zone are lower.

Because of the poor light many animals in this zone use **bioluminescence** to attract prey or mates.

Twilight zone

Ocean Layers

About 71% of Earth is covered with water and 97% of the water is in the oceans. Humans have sailed over most of it, but much of what's beneath the surface is still unexplored. The ocean depths are divided into five layers, or zones. If you passed through them you would go from light to deepest darkness, from warm to icy cold, from movement to complete stillness and from little pressure to tremendous crushing pressure.

Although some sea creatures live in several zones others inhabit only one zone. The plants and animals that live in these zones are specially adapted to their environments.

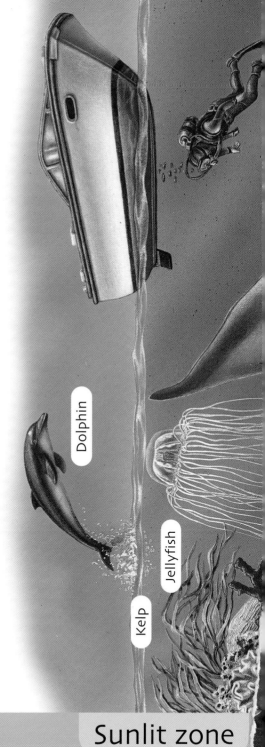

Dolphin

Kelp

Jellyfish

Sunlit zone

Beneath the Surface

In 1872 HMS *Challenger* left England on a journey to explore the world's oceans. The scientists on board wanted to find answers to questions about the depths of the oceans and what lived in them. They wanted to collect data and provide research material for the development of a new science called oceanography, the study of the oceans.

Over the next four years the scientists studied
the Pacific, the Atlantic and the Indian oceans.
They **dredged** the sea floor and discovered thousands
of previously unknown plants and sea creatures. Their
findings filled 50 volumes! An in-depth study of the
oceans had begun.

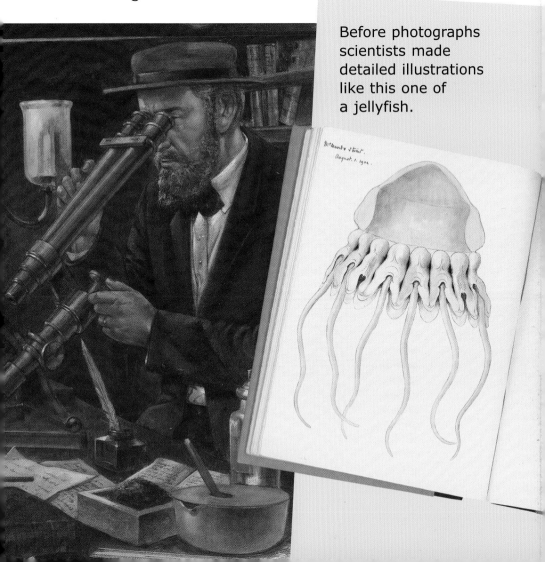

Before photographs
scientists made
detailed illustrations
like this one of
a jellyfish.

Tripod fish

Tube worms

Viper fish

Deep-sea prawn

Brittle star

In the abyss it is still, dark and very cold.

Very few creatures can survive the intense pressure, scarcity of food and total darkness of the trenches.

Abyss

Trenches

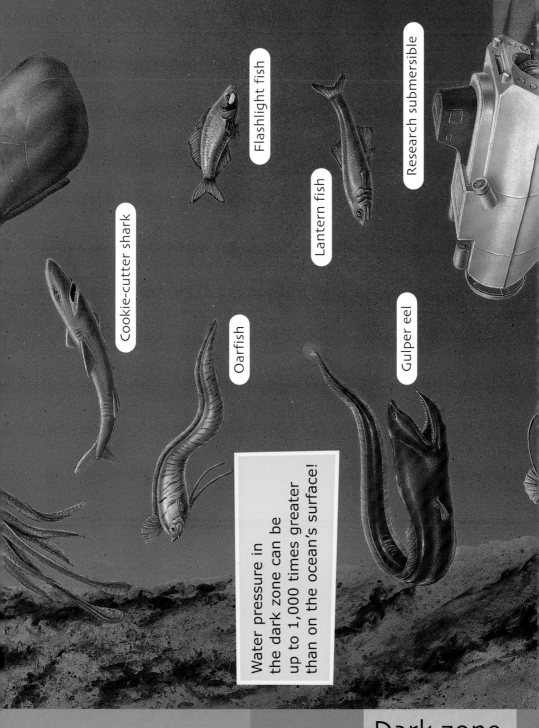

Dark zone

Predators of the Deep

Sharks are the largest of all fish. They have powerful tails and several sets of fins. Unlike other fish species sharks have flexible skeletons made from cartilage, not bone. All sharks have at least five pairs of gills so that they can breathe under water.

Classifying Sharks

Scientists organize sharks into eight extended family groups called orders. The sharks in each order share certain characteristics such as their number of gills and fins, the shape of their snouts and the way they behave.

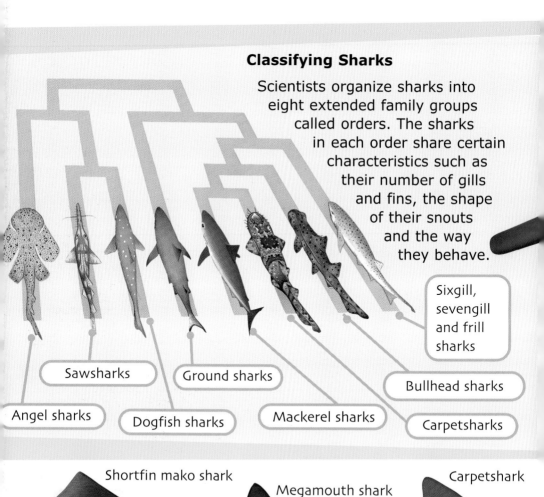

Sixgill, sevengill and frill sharks

Sawsharks

Ground sharks

Bullhead sharks

Angel sharks

Dogfish sharks

Mackerel sharks

Carpetsharks

Shortfin mako shark

Megamouth shark

Carpetshark

A great white shark can grow as long as 7 metres. Great whites are sometimes described as scavengers because they eat almost anything.

Sharks are many shapes and sizes. Some can fit in the palm of your hand while others are as big as a bus! Over thousands of years sharks have adapted to live in almost every ocean environment. To avoid competition different species hunt different prey and feed at different times of the day.

The angel shark feeds on the sea floor. It has eyes on the top of its head so it can look up to detect danger while it feeds.

Toothy Terror

Sharks are very successful predators. Not many creatures escape a hungry shark on the hunt! Many sharks have dark backs and white undersides. Seen from above or below they blend in with the water around them so they seem to swim out of nowhere to surprise their prey.

Part of the Scenery

Sharks, like many sea creatures, use **camouflage** to protect themselves or to hunt. The tassled wobbegong shark looks like a lump of seaweed. No wonder its prey can't see it coming!

What is a commonly found fossil?

Visit **www.infosteps.co.uk**
for more about **SHARKS.**

SITESEEING · PLANTS & ANIMALS ·

TRY THIS!

Hide and See

Choose a background you would like to match. Ask permission to use a safe water-based paint to make your hand blend into the background. Have a friend take a close-up photo of your hand against the background. How successful is your camouflage?

All sharks have teeth that suit the type of food they eat and the way they hunt. Sharks go through thousands of teeth in their lifetime. They usually have one row of teeth in the front biting position and a new set growing behind. As one tooth drops out another takes its place.

23

The Giants

Many people believe that all sharks are extremely dangerous. In fact only a few types of sharks are known to attack humans. Millions of people swim in the sea every day, but only about six people around the world die from shark attacks each year.

The gentle giant of the shark family is the whale shark. Growing as long as 12 metres, it looks frightening but is in fact harmless. The whale shark swims along with its huge mouth open, sucking in a living "soup" of tiny plankton, fish eggs and small fish. Then it flushes the sea water through its gill slits before swallowing the strained food.

Whale sharks eat mostly plankton and tiny fish, but they can also swallow larger fish.

The great hammerhead shark is easily recognized by the shape of its head. This giant grows to about 6 metres.

IN THE NEWS

Daily News   May 22, 2003

Giant Shark's Tooth Found

A model of the megalodon shark's jaws

A huge fossilized tooth belonging to the extinct megalodon shark has been found by a team of scientists near Norfolk Island in the Pacific Ocean.

The megalodon, or megatooth, lived millions of years ago. It grew to about 16 metres—that is three times the size of a great white shark! The megalodon's jaws would have been large enough for it to swallow a rhinoceros whole.

Saving the Whales

People have hunted whales since **prehistoric** times. At first they just killed and ate whales that became stranded on beaches, but they soon started hunting whales in the open ocean.

By the 1600s many countries had successful whaling industries and some of them have continued to this day. When the numbers of one species dropped whalers simply moved on to another species. Whaling has greatly reduced the world's whale population and pushed some species almost into extinction.

About 1,000 whales are killed each year by countries that are in favour of whaling.

The International Whaling Commission was set up in 1946 to help stop overhunting. Today most countries totally oppose whaling. Partly because of environmental organizations which have worked hard to stop whaling, there has been an international **moratorium** on whaling since 1986. A few countries, however, allow the hunting of these great creatures and put pressure on others to change their minds about the whaling issue.

WHAT'S YOUR OPINION?

I've read newspaper articles in which people who are pro-whaling say that whaling is vital for their livelihoods and an important part of their culture. I think that whales are highly intelligent animals and we should protect them. I've also read that whale numbers are still very low, although pro-whaling countries say some whale populations are high enough to cope with whaling again. The two sides seem to put forward different facts and statistics. It's difficult to know what to believe.

Preserving the Oceans

Each year there are more people on our planet who need to be fed. More and more food is taken from the oceans to feed the world's growing population. Most of the traditional fishing areas are now being **overfished** or they have reached the limits of **sustainable** fishing. Many of the world's fishing waters are also polluted.

Some countries are working to preserve the oceans by stopping pollution, limiting the number of fish that can be caught and setting up marine reserves. Fishing or hunting is not usually allowed in marine reserves so whales and other ocean dwellers can thrive. Marine reserves benefit people too. Not only do they provide people with an opportunity to see and study ocean animals, but fish numbers increase for fishing in surrounding areas.

Some Marine Reserves

North America

Europe

Asia

Africa

South America

Australia

Key ■ Marine reserve

Average Worldwide Catch per Year	
Herrings, sardines, anchovies	22,323,000 tonnes
Mackerel	5,137,000 tonnes
Shrimp, prawns	3,385,000 tonnes
Oysters	3,224,000 tonnes
Squid, octopuses	3,038,000 tonnes
Salmon, trout	2,102,000 tonnes

Whale watching has become a popular activity in many places around the world. These tourists are watching a humpback whale dive in Tonga.

Glossary

barb – a sharp point that sticks out

bioluminescence – light made by a living organism such as a deep-sea fish or a glow-worm

camouflage – colouring or covering that makes animals or objects look like their surroundings

cartilage – a strong elastic tissue that connects bones

dredge – to scrape or vacuum sand or mud from the bottom of an ocean or a river

echolocation – a system of locating objects by listening to how long a sound takes to bounce back. Bats also use echolocation.

fathom – a unit of length equal to six feet

hull – the body of a boat or ship

moratorium – a temporary ban on an activity

overfish – to take too many fish from an area so that there are few left

pack ice – huge chunks of frozen ocean water that have crushed together to become solid. Pack ice often forms at the edges of very cold countries.

prehistoric – the time before recorded history

sustainable – able to be kept going. Sustainable fishing takes limited numbers of fish, leaving enough fish to keep stocks high.

Index

Research Starters

1 Many people believe that whales are highly
intelligent animals. What do you think? Provide
some examples of whale behaviour to support
your opinion.

2 Choose a giant sea creature such as a squid,
a jellyfish or an octopus and find out more about it.
How does its size compare with the ordinary members
of its kind?

3 Cruise ships and oil tankers can also be called
"ocean giants". These huge ships can have harmful
effects on the ocean environment. Find out what some
of these harmful effects are and what is being done to
overcome them.

4 There are many stories of sea monsters that live
in the deep. Find a book of sea legends and then
retell one of the stories.